PHYSICS 1

PHYSICS THAT CALMS
THE SOUL FOR A
BETTER TOMORROW

JOHN O'DONNELL

BALBOA.
PRESS

A DIVISION OF HAY HOUSE

Balboa Press books may be ordered through booksellers or by contacting:

Balboa Press
A Division of Hay House
1663 Liberty Drive
Bloomington, IN 47403
www.balboapress.com
1 (877) 407-4847

Because of the dynamic nature of the Internet, any web addresses or links contained in this book may have changed since publication and may no longer be valid. The views expressed in this work are solely those of the author and do not necessarily reflect the views of the publisher, and the publisher hereby disclaims any responsibility for them.

The author of this book does not dispense medical advice or prescribe the use of any technique as a form of treatment for physical, emotional, or medical problems without the advice of a physician, either directly or indirectly. The intent of the author is only to offer information of a general nature to help you in your quest for emotional and spiritual well-being. In the event you use any of the information in this book for yourself, which is your constitutional right, the author and the publisher assume no responsibility for your actions.

Any people depicted in stock imagery provided by Getty Images are models, and such images are being used for illustrative purposes only.
Certain stock imagery © Getty Images.

Print information available on the last page.

ISBN: 978-1-9822-2316-8 (sc)
ISBN: 978-1-9822-2317-5 (e)

Balboa Press rev. date: 03/11/2019

PHYSICS BOOK 1

COVERS THEORIES; O'DONNELLS' CASH IDEAS IN ASTRONOMY & IDEAS ETC.

- Coding English By Monk for Physics

I need to code the English language in symbols by monks, so this book, and other O'Donnell endeavours end up funding this act first with several monasteries across the world to send to San Diego to codex. This idea is based off econometrics and might include some and might include several languages to comprise all the words needed to get to safety with ships. Ships like the Vortex Ship, Portal Layer,

THEORIES

1. Molecule Theory – This theory comprises the universe as a system in your imagination that is flung between other smaller systems in a greater system, we might call a universe once more. Using Human Duty, we can achieve the goal of colonizing this New Gaea.

2. Human Duty Theory –

    a. We might be able to use growth to achieve the goal of colonizing giant stars in the systems above, below, or around us that are about us.

    b. Also we need to work on nature resistance in the following ways

        i. Work on smoking a cigarette a day (gleaned with the help of the military) in order to achieve carbon breathing and oxygen breathing and dual breathing. Believe that there are ways to eat stars biologically and subsist on nuclear energy at its purest forms and in rough space travel. Imagine that some people are psychic in the future and can move clouds and shape the galaxy with energy from thought and move planets.

        ii. Work on nature resistance by frost training yourself in cold environments until you need a t-shirt at freezing temperatures, or shirt off in freezing after working out.

        iii. Work on heat resistance by spending a summer or better two or best three in a hot, hot environment that is baking hot in the summer for 3 months inescapably, bring a friend please to survive better - bring a dog to fight off predators – remember water and gut instincts – don't eat cactus. Detergent to clean your clothes.

3. Guzman Theory - If gravity does not escape the black hole enigma, I theorize that space and time compacts around the focus point. According to Molecule theory the black hole is a disappearing neutron sucked into a 'compound' or is en route to processing of a new system or compound on a different plane having torn the fabric of space. Riding takes

you forward in time in any direction, and the "disappearing/teleporting" black star then becomes a proton in a different molecule flung by super magnetism becoming 'charged' by crashing into or collecting space dust and fueling up for another shot at life by becoming 'positively charged.' The pathway of the flung 'neutron' or soon 'proton' becomes a Space River according to my theories, a narrow one.

4. Teleportation Feature of Molecule Theory – Carter Theory – According to Molecule Theories Stars are varying sized Neutrons and will snap into other fields of time, thus they ALMOST virtually teleport, additionally I suspect that nothing teleports, but moves at max speed light +

5. Giant Sun Theory – Deborah Theory - In one direction there is a giant sun because; I postulate that because air becomes light and thin in space and turns into time, and bigger Molecules appear looking into time, bigger and bigger, and compound looking nebulae, then in directions and certainly one direction there is a GIANT SUN/PLANET we revolve around a sun, we're flung through the heat and fusion of a GIANT SUN/PLANET in arcs and molten Space Rivers of 'hot molten goo,' inn one direction. In the other direction there is increased gravity and a big planet hosting this system as air. In addition, I postulate separately that our duty as humans is to grow ever larger to settle that found planet if planet or escape the sun in the other direction. And thus, I pinpoint our location in the Universe/ System as somewhere in the stratosphere of another planet in Molecule Theory.

6. Revision of Time Theory – Irish Theory - Time is both a solid and almost absence of everything according to Molecule Theory because the stars present an object, time is space, and there is object in space, and it's a solid because I postulate black holes tear the magnetism in space to catapult itself to another system tearing the fabric of time.

7. Die of Time Theory- O'Neil Theory– past to future, and Sun (side), a trap to Planet (side), bigger (Gaea) – Space note, Sun side and Planet side is the proper way to dock

   a. Three more direction of time on the die o' time and we don't know function

8. Time Theory – Templar (Catholic) Theory - Time is both a solid and almost absence of everything according to Molecule Theory because the stars present an object, time is space, and there is object in space, and it's a solid because I postulate black holes tear the magnetism in space to catapult itself to another system tearing the fabric of time. Time has it bits of stuff in it and sometimes bigger stuff in it, and we shrink and grow to fly/ hover through time.

9. Coding English by Monks – John's Code – Done by Monks with the capital Monetary in San Diego, monasteries in allied countries across the world. Useful for creating and perfecting a new physics based off the old one, and adding code of space to formulas in space.

10. The Universe of Universes Theory – Tamsin Theory – Tamsin, the Universe of Universes contains a Sun, and a Earth that is habitable by O-zoning it and summoning weather with star collectors collecting water on a moon/Earth close enough to the new sun. The new sun is unnamed but shall be called Sub-prime Sun for now, the Earth being called Sub-prime Earth.

11. The proximity rule Theory to the Tamsin Theory (Universe of Universes Theory), and bolstering Molecule Theory; is where there is one there is many, and certainly one next to it. Like in Molecules there is a neutron and a proton, a sun and a moon, there may be one, but there is another. Thus this universe of universe is known as Tamsin encompassing all the universe and the equivalent protons and electrons of space how ever much it may bulk up the universe with systems and galaxies.

12. The Second Universe Theory, Ashley Theory, where there is one there is many says Molecule Theory and so the universe next to the Tamsin

13. Spray Can Theory – Nancy Theory – Upgraded Big Bang Theory – All stars spray outward like from an aerosol can not unlike the cloud from a nuclear explosion, but certainly not like dynamite or nitroglycerin.

14. Fusion Theory - I propose, based off the immense number of fission America (neutron) stars, we are in a nuclear molecule (molecule theory) maybe – this is _____ or result (a), and probably a missing side to O'Neill the die of time, or we are in another Universe with an Earth because God gives us nothing we can overcome and we use human duty to Enlarge – or (b)

15. System Rearranger / Time Limitation Theory – I postulate that without going on a ride in a black hole following an almost teleporting Proton or Electron Star in order to slow down star from abroad, by using Japanese and American technology to contain a space in a room and manipulate the object inside in a part of space slowed down in the fabric of time by using gravity and possibly magnetism.

    a. A system rearranger thus contains a different space post in constant communication with the dominant space company of the time to slow down and contract manipulation of time and rearrange systems contained in a room or warp field

16. Electron Star Theory – Trump Star - A de-charging star sucking up energy from space

17. Infinite Energy Theory – I propose a few theories

    a. A particle collider in two, in the shape of Infiniti that separates helium molecules perpetually and siphons the gravitational and electrical pull to come back together to create infinite energy once started.

b. A biological organism that eats a specific fuel that can be perpetually fed and churns out light or heat or magnetic force from within that propels ships, and charges other organisms that also operate as engines by proxy and tesla-like energy transmission.

18. U.S.A. Theory – I theorize that in the future we will spot ourselves in the future and might glean off the information about what went wrong, and we have one shot to see it, and one shot to avoid what happened going wrong, because something might go wrong

    a. We spot ourselves once, unless we travel in two directions
    b. We can change what happens to ourselves once to avoid that fate
    c. We are going to space to survive a sun explosion and implosion and warping elsewhere by riding a black hole

        i. What if we ride a black hole in the wrong direction
        ii. Possibly is a black hole a last resort out?
        iii. Do we calculate in our direction the place with the most black holes as an out?

The hope of humanity:

        i. According to molecule theory, and my hypothesis of being in an immense nuclear molecule a result of time travel and 13. Fusion Theory
        ii. According to molecule theory, we might be in a biological organism, probably blood, being part of the God side of 13. Fusion Theory

It might be belief but the likelihood is that our directions that we take lead us to the right location and we probably are inside of a bloodstream of an organism.

Gleaned off the military there appears an image of a humanoid on plasma, brain molecules; now how about we be enlarged that size eventually to get on brain plasma.

Imagine, would be have to inhabit a brain molecule at the same time as possessing the ability to possess and invade the organism that keeps a brain artificially alive?

Communication is always necessary for that, and any desirable outcome across all distances, meaning an infestation everywhere always of humans. Some people will always die of a ferocious attack.

Maybe death needs to be religious like Bushido in Japan the country. We can then accept and be ready for space colonization.

Famous Quote of John's O'Donnell Jr.:

CASH IDEAS

Abstinence is the best method of life when your single. So people learn to fly like birds a monogamous and maybe pertinent adaptation, not mentioned in Human Duty.

The following contains the ideas of Prince in America and King in Ireland, John O'Donnell Jr.' mind – and O'Donnell Kingdom family property, allies, and friends.

Japan Sandwich – Two Bacon on Philadelphia Cream Cheese and red pepper with parmesan sprinkled on an open-faced wheat bread – The First Sandwich of the Space Age

PRIME IDEAS – AND PROPER SPACE, MOSTLY TIME, DICTION

Photon Star or 'Nippon' for short

Neutron Star of 'America' for short

Virtual teleportation or 'O-ffect/Offect' for short

Space Rivers or 'JOB' for short – Named after John Brian O'Donnell 3rd

Teleportation Circle or 'Cho-Hee Effect'

Charging Photon Star or 'Nippon Charger'

Space enigma 'Herb'

Fart Amplifying Pill – Free Upon Request (might have some amusing use in Time to fool an Alien, or propel us

Moon Telescope – O'Donnell can use only, and allies countries and friends; we need the Hubble and a moon telescope – close range calculations for Star Charts can finally be realized

Household Longevity Machine – O'Donnell only, and friends, and allied countries

Magnetism Amplifier System – O'Donnell, friends, and allied countries

Magnified Reducer System – O'Donnell, friends, and allied countries

Pizza Ravioli – TRADEMARK – O'Donnell technology brought into space so ingredients don't fly away

Hibernation Chamber – Icy, Drugged, Fed Chambo – O'Donnell and Friends Only, allied countries

One Way Shield – Good for Protecting Starships

Infogram – a picture that explains information, instead of a feeling, useful for coding English (free to the public) *These will help code English and Instagram once using infogram will help translate English into a decipherable code that we all acknowledge to help simplify physics to get us to space quicker.*

Bendy Bullet – Super dense bullet with super magnetism, pairs with Gravity Stimulator, electrically charged. *These are hyperactive bullets that get the alien.*

Gravity Stimulator – Bends a bullet around a focus point *This will help bend bullet and curve ships from an astrolabe around rocks and obstacles, and maybe work concurrently with black holes.*

Concave or convex mounds or dips catch grass seeds, curves – SCIENTIFIC DISCOVERY (free to the public), this tell us where to settle in space, eventually our psychic minds will move objects, trust in that – because I have psychic powers. *This discovery by John O'Donnell Jr. will help colonize space and for the future shape fields of wheat and grain. Small fields will be curved to retain the seed as a policy because of John O'Donnell Jr.*

Coding English By Monk for Physics – John O'Donnell Jr. TRADEMARK, Useful for creating a new physics and unlocking and correcting current physics. *This code will help get everyone off the planet, hopefully every major family has a space ship, maybe profiteering will keep that out of everyone's hands, we don't know.*

Application for Connecting Regional Flights to Major Airports – TRADEMARK. *This will help get us from space dock to space dock to space drydock, to Entoplex and to space Colosseums and Communication Centers. It will be the Uber of Space connected places and orbiting facilities.*

Gravity Road Minutemen – Repairing the Portals of Road that Expand and Contract for Ships, the portals have to expand and contract a lot and probably need oils for time travel. *These guys are the heart and soul of the game, they repair all space roads and space objects.*

Time Travel – O'Donnell friends and family, and allies only: must fly the O'Donnell banner. *O'Donnell's invented the first sensical time travel and claim the complicated process as a trademark, keeping it stable so no one goes back in time to screw people over, only forward in time and progress.*

Booster Magnets for Ships – They boost the ships through space portals, and include a kit for the side of ships. *Booster magnets should be on the side of every ship to accelerate naturally the movement of ships not only around each other but through portals and space roads to speed up.*

Portal Booster Magnets – Portals With Magnets for Space Road. *Portal booster magnets will be inside portals and inside space roads and boost ships along.*

Application for Connecting Regional Flights to Major Airports or Space Docks to Major Space Docks– TRADEMARK *This application will connect as it says docks to docks, and space airport*

Star Remnant – Washington (D.C.)– Remnants of a star. *This is vital O'Donnell discovery for pinpointing star remnants for astrolabe calculations and makes navigation easy for rough space dust navigation. Star charts will also need to plot lot's of Washington and lot's of Herb.*

Space Dock – TRADEMARK – *This is O'Donnell Property and allows the safe harbor of a ship to dock StarSide to Planet Side.*

Orbiter – A planetarium, or colosseum that floats in space that spins about a fixed point for gravity. *Needed for space potty breaks and such.*

Sub-Prime Devices For Space

Trademarked and Owned by the O'Donnell Kingdom and family.
Can be formed together by a volunteer company for a trading card game.

Space manipulator Devices – *This is a series of devices that preludes to the system rearranger, basically it is a simple device that doesn't rearrange but diverts star energy from one place to another like a joystick and a manipulator.*

Time adjuster device – *This adjusts time as needed whether analog or digitally we own the trademark until it becomes reality in the next ten years. Moves stars; where we can move it we can make time happen.*

Date setter device – *Date setter device sets a course in time, that slows you down as you travel so you end up at a time, and not a place. It is like an autopilot.*

Portal - *Portal brings you closer to heaven through portals in time, you get a speed boost and course readjustment between docks and orbiters.*

Gravity bender device – *Bends gravity around a fixed point, needed to possibly tear through the fabric of time and create a black hole. Needed for space travel, needed for capturing animals with Japanese pokeballs, needed for capturing stars and sucking enemies into black holes.*

Gravity reducer – *Needed for space warfare and slowing down enemies, needs a possible system rearranger command center or something similar, slows down missiles and slows down enemies in space making warfare a broadside of different attacks ranging from chemical to biological to nuclear to laser to magnetic.*

Gravity containment device – *Gravity containment device, a round device that builds a room around the object desired using laser lens and shrinks the room into the chamber using a gravity field, plasma chain, and ensmallenmentor. Similar to but distinct, and leaving alone the pokeball.*

Gravity booster – *A small device, round in shape, that combusts time, or uses magnetism to rein in time and tear the fabric of time having once connected the same plane of time to itself. Or it can be analog a time sped star bomb that sucks in gravity to be contained later and time slowed for later use.*

Space container Device – *Contains space and time itself and does so in a small round or oval container, useful for star collecting, storing energy for later, gathering minerals…prisoners and more if we have crime.*

Black matter container Device – *Stores black matter, or the invisible matter we cannot see or detect, somehow it contains quarks and smaller objects that we can harvest for something. The possibilities are when our technology can warp those tiny object into a ball.*

Dark matter container – *Contains dark matter, and smoothly contains it for the future and use of dark matter combustion or smoothing throughout the universe for potential galaxy creation the use is limitless.*

Dark matter extractor Device/Pump – *This leaks dark matter from its container to it's intended place of use.*

Dark matter extractor Device – *Small device letting out certain amounts of pressure of dark matter for a dark matter pump, and extractor of dark matter where it may lie as a hoover device of dark matter, a plasma chain bit funnels dark matter into a suction device.*

Star container Device – *We need these monstrous looming devices to contain stars before being towed and ensmallenmentored by a device for safe keeping using a system rearranger. When we contain stars we move energy and harvest or let go of time. Without containing stars we have no energy to move about space, this is why they are so tough and huge.*

Star tube Device – *Shifts stars through tubes to get desired velocity for time manipulation, part of tubules. Something so small can achieve a greater defense of people, and power through peace (Pelleliu) Fire all cannons!*

Dwarf to super-massive black hole star container Device – *A much larger spherical or conical shaped with detectors whether to use warp fields and time manipulators, or room projecting space containing tech. Captures all gravity containing enemies unless it's detecting photons which returns to sender. Intimidating technology keeps the people safe.*

Matrix tubules Device – *Enamallenmented rooms and stars functioning to replicate a small ecosystem to learn a program. Can be shared with Matrix Trilogy. Learning quick is both a defense and an offense, and a sharp mind wins the moment.*

Matrix tubes Device – *Small connecting tubes for different room simulation. Defense is found by exploring more space.*

Body amplifier (to survive space) Device – *Raises selected traits from a preset to withstand space biologically for a time likely at a cost to the immune system. Lowering your defense can mean temporary survival.*

Enlariger Device – *Selects the traits growth, technological, separate from the already claimed growth potion in motion by Activision, and enlargens to even the playing field. Likely combines time amplification and a system rearranger to get a unit large fast. Monsters and friends of space will wonder and be stunned by such sudden growth, consume a star and there is no need for it anymore.*

Ensmallenmentor Device – *Makes small what was normal, uses a system rearranger and a warp field around a certain area to make smaller the unit or area to journey as a pathogen in a foreign unit enemy unit or be an antibody in any unit. Use extreme measures for great offense or great defense.*

Star smelter Device - *Smelts stars analog, for safety is in machines still. Hulking, large, tedius, but towable. Creates armor, ships, and useful items. Items in great quantity allow for enhanced production when enlarging. Creates plasma chains.*

Star forge Device – *Forges in conjunction with star smelter to create the items we seek. Play the two together and you can play en-largerners and travel time quicker.*

Gravity field creation device – *Uses magnetics and/or gravity to rip a field in space or the two combined to shape a field that needs to be selected for manipulation. Control mechanism, selects units in space. Control leads to better self-sentiment, and a better defense.*

Space politics TRADEMARK for Universe 2; senate, congress, vice president and president, 99 judges for Ireland & 99 judges for America, 99 Judges for royal South Korea, 99 Judges for Europe, 99 Judges for Spain, 99 Judges for royal Iran, 99 Judges for the grand rulers in the Papacy, and 99 Judges for the royal Phillipines, and Imperial Monk Police to enforce law. *Law and order leads to better communication, communication keeps us together, and this keeps all units frosty for battle with the Gaia's unknown stories.*

Underwater Electric Billboard device – *For colonizing Jupiter and under the water in preparation for the great Sun Earth 1 swallow. Neptune and Uranus are safer with shelter. Space with shelter bolsters space politics.*

Underwater Road Device – *Underwater roads are meant to last long and underwater under specific pressures, possibly emitting to self-driving or manual option cars. Safer passageways lead to greater commerce, more money.*

Underwater Road Analog TRADEMARK - *Underwater roads are meant to last long and underwater under specific pressures.*

Underwater houseproofing TRADEMARK/Device – *Emits when soundproofing and waterproofing is damaged with a water and sonic sensor each. Proofs houses to make the place safe. Safer places make for higher productivity.*

Underwater house portal Device – *Underwater house portal is the entryway to a dwelling, make it cheap and it becomes more grand to the customer in style. Happier people lead to more commerce.*

Underwater soundproofing – *Underwater soundproofing can be interlocking pentagonal sheet metal used in favelas, or plastics, that reflect out sound simply and interlock over any underwater structure.*

Underwater house – *Made cheaply for the public to use, it enforces strong economic output and more people, with plenty of space there is plenty of commerce. You can see sharks, and make money while on terra-firma you could only see birds.*

Hand Narwhaling technique TRADEMARK to protect narwhal ivory – *Narwhaling is strictly enforced for royalty to harvest once a lifetime if necessary to pass down, and only by Beowulfing it can you obtain one. Keep the Narwhals happy, and humans can dance underwater with the Narwhal forever, for happiness.*

Plasma shield (might belong to bungie) – *A two way shield that blocks things, useful in space for dividing harsh zones for as long as the plasma holds, might be useful in eating stars for enlargened star-eaters and such.*

Force field (might belong to star wars) – *Similar to plasma shield, this can cover a town, or ship, also causing a barrier for harsh environments probably allowing to stream and swing off stars.*

Gravity field strength detector Device – *Analog is using plasma chains at a depth of fathoms, and the device uses plasma chain in a retracting magnetic gravity ball.*

Radiation amplifier Device – *Amplifies radiation using photon enhancers, gatherers and distributors and containers. Control the radiation and control the burn on your enemies.*

Radiation reducer Device (analog only might belong to NASA) – *Using photon abosorbers and photon storage radiation can be reduced. Safer means more defense throughout space.*

Radiation bender Device – *With a brilliant magnetic field, the device beds even the smallest particles. When the smallest can be redirected, all molecules can go in one direction together, for a more efficient attack, beam, energy, force, or force shield with a few spaced out.*

Radiation reduction device Device – *Photon absorbers and a photon condenser stores photons for force shields, while reducing radiation.*

Gravity simplifier Device - *Gravity becomes analog and digital one of the two, and becomes transmittable electronically.*

Gravity digitizer Device – *Another way of saying Gravity Simplifier to level the playing field for Space Company 1 that will form from the funding of this book, and investors.*

Mass digitizer Device – *Mass becomes digital for the matrix, and for experiments on stars and structures, simplifying the mass into numbers and symbols, perhaps the items can be moved digitally with further research.*

Star digitizer Device – *Digitizes stars code for the matrix, ensmallment, collecting, and transport.*

Star collector Device – *Collects stars, makes them available for energy whilst in storage and underway, ensmallenments them for storage within, discharges stars for system rearrangement in conjunction with ensmallenmentors and enlargerenmentors system rearranges. Critical tools, lessen the need for thought, and free up the imagination for readiness, a first attack.*

Star simplifier Device – *Simplifies stars down to the base, by fast forwarding, or slowing down time until it can be thrust into another star to increase processes of simplifying to a black hole or base molecules or other molecules for combustion, eating, fuel, or more.*

Battlecruiser (starcrafts) – *A really, cool concept, that I would like to see happen for humans are pretty set on the idea, with little protest.*

Nuclear cannon Device – *Similar to the Yamato cannon, and I am willing to cede the idea over to Activision. Great defense requires great energy.*

Laser ray CaNnOn Device – *Laser cannons, I postulate are cannons with charges on centrifical sides of the barrel to eventually be propelled forward in immense energy as a laser. Then we have lasers, and lasers cannons and they will rake the enemy quickly.*

Electric diffusing bomb Device – *Similar to EMP, these tiny devices can be shot with a discharge weapon to displace energy within a cannisters explosion, might be useful for future (ghost) or elite sniper units. "Diffuse the laser cannon with a squad and fire the space torpedoes. Eliminate the foreigners tech, and blast through their force shields make them fight analog." Double the attack means double the trouble.*

Star creation bomb Device – *Creates a bomb with micro-star generation using tubules and tubules of star fed tubes and creates a star out of many small ones rapidly distributed and allowed to expand at long last. Yehar matey, we sail, we made a star portside earth side and ride for the coast of the event horizon. Speediness is the way out of creating a star.*

Biological nuclear reactor fed chemical – *The limitless potential in a creature biologically cultivated over time to create energy in different formats. – Leasable since I am broke to get started, for a meager payout amongst knights and family.*

Biological nuclear reactor fed metals and nuclear waste – *Cultivated organism possibility two, leasable by the Kingdom of O'Donnell for disbursement to knights and family since we are broke – for a meager payout amongst knights and family.*

Biological creature with AC and DC output and light organ for long lasting light source to harvest energy from – *Cultivated biological creature 3, leasable under the same conditions by the O'Donnell Kingdom, for a meager payout amongst knights and family.*

Biological creature that runs on biofuel – *Biological creature 4, leasable under the same conditions, for a meager payout amongst knights and family.*

Biological creature that runs on biological food – *Biological creature 5, leasable under the same conditions, for a meager payout amongst knights and family.*

Trademark the harvesting of energy from biological energy reactor – *Think extractor, and then you have it. I cede the idea to Activision and revel in their brilliance.*

Trademark the harvesting of light from biological creature (53) – *Biological creature or adaptation 6, leasable under meager payouts and similar conditions for my knights.*

Rock container w/ time amplifier – *A device comprised of technology once created above, to amplify time quickly to get to diamonds or certain gems, with my discovery and proof that gems come from compacted petrified wood, and produce gold and quartz to harder gems.*

Geode imploder Device – *Implodes rocks and geodes to harvest the inside in a container, that looks like pistons shooting into the inside of a hollowed sphere alternatingly.*

Rock emulsifier Device – *Emulsifies rock, to make lava, and create liquid energy for some future purpose, possibly feeding biological organisms.*

Rock implosion machine with ground injectors – *Implodes ground with diamond sharp injector steam driven or hydraulically driven into the ground with harvesters on the back and in the future containment devices with ensmallenmentors, or emulsifiers to separate the goods. Designed for maximum rock harvesting. Harvest quick, build fast, build two objects instead of one.*

Rock eater with nuclear containment device – *Nuclear powered and gathered rock eater, gathering all ores even tougher mineral.*

Blast and hydroproof living module – *Living madules increase commerce, we need more space Lord.*

Blast and hydroproof and flameproof living module – *Key to colonizing space and Jupiter, and underwater lands, Neptune and Uranus and Earth and Mars. Increased habitation equals increased commerce.*

Solar array hydro and blast proof – *Extreme weather solar arrays for space cocolonization of Jupiter and underwater surfaces, increased commerce comes from organized energy generation.*

Rock container w/ time reducer Device - *Slows down passage of time, to get the particles just right in a gem. Increased commerce from perfect gems backing cash in conjunction with gold and silver.*

Analog gravity detector - *Uses a star or super magnetized ore on a meter to detect faint gravity with analog in case the ships were hit by an Electronic diffuser.*

Analog gravity reducer – *Uses a star or super magnetized ore to reduce gravity with analog in case the ships were hit by an Electronic diffuser.*

Ensmallment chamber Device – *A chamber to gradually ensmallen and diminish humans or organisms, using noble gas and other devices mentioned. Greater defense comes in small forms to fight pathogens or infect an enemy.*

Enlargement chamber Device – *A chamber to gradually amplify and enlarge humans or organisms, using noble gas and other devices mentioned. Greater offense comes in collecting stars in size and enlargening throughout space. Cutting the enemy down with a sword instead of a cannon.*

Battle room (might belong to Marvel, sorry Marvel) – *Practice room enlargened or ensmallened to contain the necessary digitized warfare for practice amongst psychic and mechanical troops.*

Space collesseum – *A collesseum free to public and government, or perhaps contributed to by the O'Donnell for sentenced space battles and glorified war to satisfy the need for entertainment live in space, and keep tactics sharp using all spectrums of war.*

Artificial planet (excluding halo shape) -

Space platform Device (excluding artificial halo planets) – *Breaks between space where one can stop so you can pee and revel in space, perhaps using a amplifier or two, or taking one of O'Donnell's war or peace drug technology.*

Space road trademark, light portals - *Potentially magnet/magnetized infused roads that propel equally equipped spaceships to travel at a faster guided computer analyzed speed and trajectory. Made to be manipulated in size for large ship and small in the future so magnets have a better use for different sizes.*

Space NASSHIP (like nascar) – *Ship racing of the future*

Space Drydock – *A orbiting or stationary space drydock made from tons of earth materials and mineral ore for repairing giant sized and pint sized ships, family ships and battle ships.*

Star containment energy siphoner Device – *Once contained the device siphons the dormant energy of a compacted star that cannot expand much, and the energy flows in plasma or light through conductors to a furnace burning for energy. Near infinite energy creates boundless experiments in the quest for infinite energy and propels it further.*

Magnet Turbo Thruster Device – *Revolving magnets spin higher velocities at lower friction making faster rockets and better combustion. Fast ships, is faster time travel, is a better offense, and a fly's defense when played one at a time.*

Item Enlarger Device - *Enlarges items, in conjunction to the ensmallenmentor, literally compacts the molecules to shrink it using a variety of means instead of permanent system rearrangement to a congruent size.*

Item Shrinker Device – *Shrinks items, in conjunction to the ensmallenmentor, literally compacts the molecules to shrink it using a variety of means instead of permanent system rearrangement to a congruent size.*

Mindset Changer Device – *Rearranges mindsets based on our knowledge of the human brain, may belong to Einstein. Useful for altering the mind for good, longer term benefits, larger or lower hormones, and growth potential. Used once in one way, enhances defense or offense in a given play on the field and game of life.*

Molecule Rearranger Device – *System rearranger ensmallenmented for rearranging molecules quickly, dense to light, noble to liquid. If the table is liquid and the food becomes solid, surprise is ours.*

System Rearranger Device – *Device connects to all bullets and all system rearrange posts for communication of the needs to system rearrange.*

System Rearranger bullets and varieties Device – *Bullets tipped with a trigger to the system rearranger command post in a warped time fabric of space in a near teleported distance. These bullets are the ultimate offense, rearrange a liver with a heart and drop the bodies. Useful on large and small organisms.*

System Rearranger bomb and varieties – *System rearranger bomb tears through a group of enemies or solar systems based on size and from a system rearranger command post the workers rearrange the system or bodies using medical or star collector technology.*

Fast Motion Field Device - *System rearranger using near teleportation to achieve a system rearranger command post, allows you to fast motion by containing a warp field around the object desired to fast motion, requires lock-on technology and gravity and magnetic field booster devices to create a containment for time folding time fabric.*

Fast Motion Device Device – *System rearranger using near teleportation to achieve a system rearranger command post, allows you to fast motion by warp-teleporting through time to a slower region of folded space and thus increases time for manipulating the warp field back into place.*

Slow Motion Field Device – *Another broad ranged slow-motion device used for larger things like stars and black holes and things that need slowing down. What happens if you slow-down seeming teleportation, can you communicate or attack through it?*

Slow Motion Device Device – *Slow motion device needs a system rearranger command post in a different area of space at the least, and slows down a range of time in a warp field*

Magnetic Body Shredder Device – *Needed, for eviscerating biological enemies in space. Bug, humanoid, or animalinoid.*

Magnetic Fielderizer – *Turbo charge the magnetic field in a device, absorb the tiniest photons. Control is defense.*

Item Enlarger Device – *Enlarges analog or digitally using afore or post mentioned technology. What remains is a liquid energy feeder that biologically attached onto material to enhance compounds in a system in all directions congruently.*

Item Shrinker Device - *Enlarges analog or digitally using afore or post mentioned technology. What remains is a liquid energy feeder that biologically attached onto material to diminish compounds in a system in all directions congruently.*

Mindset Changer Device – *Already exist, consists of using waves on studied materials of brains in animals to evoke certain emotions, pain, or happiness, or feelings or whatever one wishes in the future. I cede to whoever owns it, but agree it is important for attack and defense.*

Molecule Rearranger Device – *Bolsters System Rearranger Trademark*

System Rearranger Device – *A device thrown or shot inside a bullet that triggers in the magnetic field of the recipient a near freeze in time and a rearrangement of tissue to form around the bullet to heal fast or brace for it, in addition to changing it's components all the way up to in size of a solar system, galaxy, or universe as technology grows. Should psionic energy not suffice to rearrange the stars and heavens.*

System Rearranger bullets and varieties Device – *System rearrangers in the tip of a bullet spear round. Attack on a grand scale.*

System Rearranger bomb and varieties – *System rearranges with a bomb size to arrange and rearrange using known technology to change a system for the better or worse. Attack and defense on a grand scale.*

Fast Motion Field Device – *Speeds up warfare and obstacles. Attack boost.*

Fast Motion Device Device – *Speeds up using known technology with a handheld device in the future, bolstering the Fast Motion Field Device TRADEMARK.*

Slow Motion Field Device

Slow Motion Device Device – *Slows up using known technology with a handheld device in the future, bolstering the Slow Motion Field Device TRADEMARK.*

Fast Motion Bomb – *Fast motions anything in a radius for a consumed mini-star amounts of time and speeds up the decay and attack of things within the field of effect.*

Slow Motion Bomb – *Slow motions anything in a radius for a consumed mini-star amounts of time and speeds up the decay and attack of things within the field of effect.*

Analog Change Trademark – *Analog Change is made through giant leaps in space as machinery grows every larger to be detected with a mere telescope in the past, Starside, Planetside, or any other direction on the O'Niell, die of time.*

Star-collection Trademark-*Star collection is a past/present/and future hobby of Earthlings and humanoids of Earth as we scramble outward for resources consuming and gathering momentum as we stay in communication to enter a direction or all directions of time for sustenance.*

Cocaine Island Trademark – *A novelty TRADEMARK to keep all production of Cocaine safe, and engineered properly for medicine and health benefits for daily injectors to light users not addicts, users.*

Underground Highways – *TRADEMARK – Highly coveted O'Donnell technology that we will rent out at meager wages to Governments around the world to connect countries and subvert the oceans to colonize underwater and become united with Gaia. Gaia victory points, commerce increase*

Legal Unions – *A space entity of legal workers, semi royalty, who through guidance of the Royals around the world exercise a union eventually for not regulating income and world prices but for self-sustenance as the need for politicians and knightly duty increases.*

Proton Extractor Device – *Extracts with tender machine care, protons from molecules and protons from star systems for certain applications like creating energy or infinite energy under O'Donnell's' infinite energy theory.*

Universe Creator – *Using psionic energy in the vast future, how one might postulate pyramids were built, universes can get shaped. Conversely using machinery in a system of technology the universe is a giant system and old stars can be harvested or repurposed if not eaten for sustenance by biological infinite energy organisms we cultivate. Star collectors are vital, and giant tow devices.*

Forward Astrolabe Device - *Floats forward by magnetism ahead of a ship to transmit details of space and conditions back to the ship for movement, can be replaced if hit, initializes force shields, and more in emergency and detects gravity to shift position.*

Item Projector Device – *Projects an item in theory, to transmit in the matrix and eventually in life items of interest, gold, silver, platinum, bronze etc. and weapons and tools at a cost of energy that likely grows smaller in time.*

Molecule Arranger Device – *System rearranger,* shrunk down and microtized.

Voting system that works from Apple IStore or Android Google Play - You vote bi-weekly on new laws, you get up to date rulings from Senate and Congress or Space Congress, and in this way Space Congress get's formed (see previous post 99 seats Japan, 99 Seats Ireland, 99 Seats U.S., 99 Seats S. Korea, 99 Seats Philippines, Queen of England 99 Seats, and Iceland 99 Seats, Greenland 99 Seats, and Canada 99 Seats, Mexico 99 Seats, Under Monroe Doctrine, South America 99 Seats, Germany and the Union 99 Seats, China 99 Seats, Russia 99 Seats, Middle East 249+ Seats, India 99 Seats, South East Asia 99 Seats- *laws are introduced by the O'Donnell family and are voted in to vote by congress and the senate and the people every 2 weeks, important core laws are refreshed every year, and semi important laws that we categorize as such are important enough to vote on and refresh every two years.*

Dance Website Connecting Choreographers and Dancers and Making art Plentiful - *Dances get posted and stuff – Culture Increases*

Item Projector Device – Item projector projects the item simulated and thrusts it through time having bound the fabric of time of two places temporarily, might consume a lot of energy.

Molecule Arranger Device – System rearranger shrunk down

Molecule Lens Device – Someone tell me why I invented this and email me at mainodonnell@ protonmail.com

Molecule Projector Device – Using an item projection device microtized, this projects

Compound Absorber – *Assists and bolsters the TRADEMARK of Coumpound Tightener for storage/ shrinkage of items or youth and longevity.*

Compound Tightener – *Tightens skin and other compounds for storage/shrinkage or youth and longevity*

Time Recorder (not like the memory recorder in Rick and Morty) – *In theory, records time, and allows the manipulation of it's fabric in the future kept safe by the Royal O'Donnell Family kept safe by Roman Catholic Templar.*

Time Absorber – *Attracts with gravity time fabric for manipulation, in theory.*

Photon Attractor – *Attracts photons with magnetism.*

Female Pleasure Device Expanding in the Vagina and Twisting Around – *Increased Happiness and Commerce*

Adrenaline, Methamphetamine, Anabolic Steroid Compound Injectable – *Health bonus, Defense Up*

Adrenaline, Mephedrone, Anabolic Steroid Compound Injectable - *Health bonus, Defense Up*

Refrigerated Soil Trademark – *In conjunction directly with Baron Ryan of El Centro and Ireland, this technology brings health benefits to certain crops, indirectly and less-so happiness and commerce*

Drug Union trademark- *Legalizes under royalty drugs, and soon worldwide for the health and happiness benefits and intelligence boosts likely. Unions will become the kingpins that deal with government directly to supply and tax for them with charters issued by the secretary of Offense in John O'Donnell Jr.'s Royal Presidency and soon following Kalen O'Donnell 1ˢᵗ Royal Presidency as to reduce corruption we rule together with an option of who to pay tax to, to reduce corruption and increase participation.*

Secret Technology Blank Spot – *Insert your own invention here*

_____/_____

Methamphetamine Creme, and 3.1) Heroin Crème – *Wartime peacetime medicine, Defense up, Happiness up*

.

Chlorine Artificial Smell to disguise wartime smells – *Fog of war technique and TRADEMARK. Attack and defense goes up.*

Flowchart program trademark for business – *Trademark to make business fun, a website of sorts to help business flow forward and programs easier to introduce.*

Photon Vacuum – *Uses a further mentioned tech, to suck up photons, and gather them using tubules for condensing and storage probably for use in force shields.*

Photon Condensor – *Condenses and cools using tubules and small gravitational traps within the tubules to condense photons for storage.*

Photon Containment – *Storage using a space container, or room ensmallenmentor, or other such conjunction of devices rapidly to cool down and contain photons.*

Gravity Booster – *Boosts gravity with a certain wavelength material, and digitally it reads the sources and blasts out a higher overwhelming frequency.*

Gravity Condenser – *Condenses gravity digitally and analog with certain material and a digitized for the matrix.*

Gravity Amplifier - *Condense gravity analog by setting up a creating of stars or imploding or artificial black hole with timed stars using a system rearranger. And then Digitally such as well.*

Sex room trademark – *Happiness increases with commerce*

Sex rock- *Happiness increases with commerce*

Sex couch from stone - *Happiness increases with commerce*

Sex ottoman from stone - *Happiness increases with commerce*

Sex stone furniture - *Happiness increases with commerce*

3" drug sniffer- *Happiness increases with commerce.*

Gravity Condensor – *Condense gravity analog by setting up a creating of stars or imploding, inside of a condenser or use them for a black hole for more, or digitally and with a device by amplifying magnetism waves by absorbing photons in a controlled star explosion.*

Miniature Electrical Amplifier – *Amplifies signals to the edges of the universe or within a warp field using tesla technology and modern advances with given energy sources. I cede the property to the current owner.*

Chlorine Bullets – *Munitions. Defense. Offense.*

Sarin Bullets– *Munitions. Defense. Offense.*

Gas Bullets Trademark– *Munitions. Defense. Offense.*

HIV Bullets– *Munitions. Defense. Rarely Offense, except for Space alien issues.*

Gas munitions– *Munitions. Defense. Offense.*

Compound Absorber Cream For Skin and Vagina – *Longevity tool. Health up of citizenry, happiness up, and commerce up*

Compound tightener cream for skin and vagina – *Longevity tool. Health up of citizenry, happiness up, commerce up*

Nautical Schoolhouse – *Health up of citizenry*

Underwater traffic light – *Health up of citizenry*

Underwater yield sign -*Health up of citizenry*

Underwater signage – *Health up of citizenry*

Underwater Colosseum – *Bolsters happiness of citizenry*

Underwater bath house – *Bolsters health of citizenry, happiness and commerce as a forum*

Fog of war control room Trademark – *Bolsters the fog of war idea of cannister supply ships and satellite supply/cannister drops. Attack and defense amplified.*

Fog of war controller trademark – *Bolsters the Trademark of the Control room, Bolsters Defense and Attack.*

Fog of war program – *A program to solidify and bolster the TRADEMARK of a fog of war map interaction device,. War boosted on all sides.*

Fog of war map interaction device – *A magnetic coordinated machinery analog, or device that manipulates fog of war at coordinates to work in EMP shocks offline or online with electricity to command legions of command centers where to advise attention. War boosted on all sides.*

LABRADOR RETRIEVER DOGGIE DILDO☺ – *Important as our canine friends glean information off of us with doggie brain modifier tubules and modification technology. Commerce. Attack. Increases commerce slightly, culture.*

Moats – *Defense, nobody trademarked moats yet. "Irish moat victory, just kidding."*

Super Duper Bullet Maul – *Infuses bullets into mauls, attacks.*

Electric Maul – *Infuses electric into mauls, attack and defense.*

Nitrogen Cold Maul – *Infuses cold into attacks and defense with nitrogen and colder elements. Attack and defense.*

Fire-blast maul - *Infuses fire into attacks using nitrogen and other explosive elements, increases attack.*

Trademark selling offshore property to raise funds for the deficit – *Commerce, culture*

Timestamp – *Culturally relevant information that marks the time in a book, culture.*

Fog of war Manipulator Gun GPS Oriented

Fog of war Command Center Trademark – *Contemplation zone for dropping supplies and cannisters of gasses to manipulate fogs of war.*

Fog of war cannisters – *Takes the glory to the next level. Commands attention, fear, and response from the enemy to bunch them, and spread them at will for the most dominant manipulator. "Fear is the least worry, manipulation is the greatest fear."*

EMP Flak Cannon – *Takes out the electrical gauges and machinery, and leaves analog alone. Attack.*

Elephant Special Forces/ Peacekeepers Trademark- *Defense, Culture, Commerce, Gaia Victory Point*

Underwater Train Trademark - *Commerce*

Underwater Rail Cars - *Commerce*

Bridge to Hawaii to Japan, China and Phillipines - *Commerce*

Cocaine Syringe – *Commerce (timestamp English device, records date in time by reference of technology)*

Kingdom Presidency Rule trademark – *Commerce, Culture*

Space Torpedo – *Attack.*

Honey Fries Trademark (Honey fries) - *Culture*

Maple Syrup Fries Trademark (Canadian Fries) - *Culture*

Space Embargo War Tactic Trademark - *Culture*

Pesto French Fries with Parmesan (Italian Fries) - *Culture*

French Fry Cookbook TRADEMARK – *Culture, requires two or more fries collected*

Space Fries – TRADEMARK – *Culture, injected fries with meats and sauces*

Skullolio, Skull Portfolio of Tattoos in California and Mexico (in progress) BOOK IDEA TRADEMARK - *Culture*

Rappin this: "I ain't a sucka, your Momma is a ducka, I call her mine, 'cuz I make her whine." – *Culture*

Anti-radiation poisoning technique manual, fighting Americas Doomsday device manual trademark (book in progress) - *Commerce*

Echo Meditation technique that O'Donnell's mastered, TRADEMARK – *Free of charge, purifies thoughts for commerce.*

Kingdom of O'Donnell TRADEMARK - *Commerce*

Ray Cannon W/ Multiple Targeting – *Uses centrifugally powered rays from barrels to target multiple targets using homing or remote activated cannons for an instant fight. Commerce at collesseum.*

Anti-gravity Weapon Return With Hand Sensors and Weapon Sensors – *Uses magnets to grip weapons and similarly imbued weapons systems. Defense, keeps weapons gripped, and weapons mounted.*

Weapon Sensors – *Defense, keeps weapons gripped.*

Hand Weapon Sensor - *Defense, keeps weapons gripped.*

Sensor Control Room Trademark – *Defense, keeps weapons gripped.*

Shoulder Mounted Revolver w/ Auto Lock from Control Room – *Attack.*

Body Mounted Weapons System Control Room – *Defense and Attack. The best peace comes through power. – Peleliu commander Schnell Dynasty*

Body Mounted Weapons Systems Elite Soldiers w/ Control Room Analysis Trademark – *Defense or Attack, the best peace comes through power. -Peleliu commander Schnell Dynasty*

Shoulder Mounted Sonic Beam- *Attack. Requires communication.*

Shoulder Mounted Gravity Beam – *Attack. Requires communication.*

Chest Mounted Sonic Beam – *Attack. Requires communication.*

Chest Mounted Gravity Beam – *Attack. Requires communication.*

Bulletproof Space Helmet – *Defense. Requires communication.*

Bulletproof/Fireproof/Radio wave Proof Space Helmet – *"Defense, defense and more defense." Commander shouted, "get defense cubed on those soldiers and send them out against the incoming onslaught." Defense comes in all forms, no pun intended.*

Space Helmet Mounted Mini Rocket Revolver - *It's a platform mounted mini rockets revolving on space helmetes for defense in intimate combat, ran by programming or a remote team in a command post. More defense comes from immense defense per square inch.*

Space Helmet Mini Revolver Mount - *It's a platform mount for mini revolvers or mini rockets on space helmets for defense in intimate combat, ran by programming or a remote team in a command post. More defense comes from immense defense per square inch.*

Space Helmet Mini Revolver Platform – *It's a platform mounting mini revolvers on space helmetes for defense in intimate combat, ran by programming or a remote team in a command post. More defense comes from immense defense per square inch.*

Satellite and/or Supply Dropship – *Drops items and cannisters of fog of war to manipulate battle in a mobile command post. "Tell the royal commander to drop supplies and mask the gathering." We gathers defense to control the fog of war.*

Satellite Cannister Drop Trademark- *Armor for troops. Defense comes in armor. "Control the fog of war, drop cannisters to mask troop positions."*

Nationwide PA System and Intercom w/ Microphone - *Armor for troops. Defense comes in armor.*

Bulletproof/Fireproof/Radio Wave Proof Space Suit – *Armor for troops. Defense comes in armor.*

Sewn Together Mutant Zombie Soldiers Trademark – *biological research creation that will tear apart enemies through force and fear. Increased attack dramatically.*

Mutant Zombie Soldiers Trademark– *Zombie soldiers dropped from hell, they act without fear and zeal of Holy Monks, bolsters sewn together mutant zombie soldier trademark. Increased attack dramatically.*

Overmind Organism Interactor w/ Computer Control – *Organism that controls and distributes energy psionic or otherwise amongst creature biologically cultivated and more.*

Computer Hologram Keyboard W/ Hologram Keys – *Better commerce, better computers.*

Dog Control Implant – *Implant containing the matrix and various learning programs to allow another field of memory in dogs. More allies, more attack.*

Dog Control Program – *A program of research attempting to control dogs with an implant to teach using the matrix and enhance them as humanoids or animalinoids. More allies, double the attack.*

Druid Trademark Master of Nature – *Potentially O'Donnell's, willing to share with Activision for contributions to Science. Druid people, summoners of weather and psyonic energy. Similar to high-templars in Starcraft.*

Mutant Creature Troop Carriers for Space – *Gleaned from Starcraft, definitely possible, go Activision.*

Waffle Hotdog Trademark – Sell to Roscoes Chicken and Waffles, Ketchup and Mustard infused Weiner – *Space food, increased happiness*

Space Birthing Chamber – *Allows sex and reproduction in space. Mo-mo- people…mo-mo-money.*

Oxy/Opioid Suppository – *Makes the go better, happy people creates more commerce.*

Ninja Star That Releases Microscopic Bullets on Impact – *Better attack*

Ninja Star That Releases a Bomb on Impact Delayed or Instant – *Better attack*

Ninja Star That Electro Shocks – *Better attack*

Ninja Star That Freezes the Tissue – *Better attack*

90% tobacco 10% Methamphetamine Smokable Product

90% tobacco 10% Opioid smokable product

Maple Syrup Philadelphia Cream Cheese

Maple Syrup Butter w/ a Maple Syrup Paste in the Butter

Maple Syrup Margarine

Radio Wave Proof Inter/Intra Stellar Ship Armor

TRADEMARK (might piss people off) Re-coining Americas Gold and Silver Policy since inflation is out of control and soldiers and agents make less than a skilled worker, my knowledge my idea, maybe I'll profit off it but I will probably donate it to the poor. And recoining under using gemstones. *Self-explanatory, increases commerce, more money is more commerce.*

Opioid Coffee Rods – *Future tech, happier people creates more money circulating.*

Opioid Wine – *Future tech, happier people creates more money circulating.*

Xanax Coffee Rods – *Future tech, happier people creates more money circulating.*

Cocaine Coffee Rods – *Cocaine coffee rods, the best of both worlds, happier people creates more money circulating.*

Cocaine Wine - *Happier people creates more money circuating.*

Cocaine/Amphetamine/Mephedrone Injection Battle Booster Primarily/ Death Drug – *Used by troops and royal Monks and knights alike, creates a reason to fight and a reason to work harder – stimulates commerce through competition.*

Space Fishing Lure – *Uses a clamp of three different sizes to hold onto meat chunks and has two hooks or any number of useful hooks, for all baits instead of irregular shapes only usable on old lures. Creates more money circulating, happier people.*

IDEAS GIVEN AWAY TO GOVT.

Minutemen – Gov't. Idea, Gleaned in Cooperation w/ Military Gleaning Off My Work, they can have it

Footnote: NASA's Mars grow room was copied from my orbiting space grow room that is towable because the government issued the publication on twitter days after I published my space grow room on Facebook, lawsuit pending. Proof that the Patriot Act is being misused by our government to spy on high profile people. I never gave permission to be spied on, but my work gets copied or stolen by military intelligence all the time…so I publish right away on Twitter or Facebook. It just goes to show people that Twitter and Facebook aren't safe from the government, the government run by "trumpo," steals ideas from my space knowledge and alters it to try and make it their own, but it is too similar to a grow facility in space to be theirs published one day after. And I have a lawsuit against the Presidency, which makes this surveillance a terrorist act of t he government, and this text a publication of the legal President before being recognized.

IDEAS STOLEN THUS FAR BY GOVERNMENT

Entoplex – Stolen on twitter days after I published it to Facebook (proving they follow me illegally and other genius citizens farming their technology, Nick Monterrey shutout)

One Way Shield – Stolen many days after publishing to Facebook

Proving once again the government follows citizens and steals from the best and brightest. Not to worry Mr. McDermott Esq. of Palm Springs is defending our space property that I hold for freedom so no government can bully anyone.

Printed in the United States
By Bookmasters